WHAT PEOPLE ARE SAYING ABOUT

Guiding Children Through Life's Losses

"Guiding Children Through Life's Losses is an enchanting and enhancing look at many ordinary and extraordinary life events that drag children out of their safe cocoons and into the harsh realities of what the world can be. Without safe surroundings children suffer needlessly and in isolation. This book offers hands-on activities that are as important to the adults who share and present them as to the children who will both receive and give.

"This book will be a comfortable fit in the home and classroom, in parishes of all sizes and shapes, and especially in the worship and learning ministries of the church. The latter setting is crucial, for this book will be an informed wake up call to the churches who so often offer only meager bereavement care at best, and generally only for the adults. When used with care, this resource will open up many wounds, scars, stories, and even dreams. Read and use this gift wisely, but also pay close attention to your own grief issues."

—The Very Rev. Richard B. Gilbert
Executive Director, The World Pastoral Care Center
Author and Presenter on bereavement and
pastoral care issues, including *Kids Grieve*

"Wonderful, well done, and needed! Christian schools should be the best at dealing with children's losses and other heartaches. At last help has arrived. This carefully crafted material beautifully meets a never-ending need."

—James R. Kok
The Crystal Cathedral

Guiding Children
through
Life's Losses

Prayers, Rituals & Activities

Phyllis Vos Wezeman • Jude Dennis Fournier
Kenneth R. Wezeman

TWENTY-THIRD PUBLICATIONS
Mystic, CT 06355

Second printing 2001

Twenty-Third Publications
A Division of Bayard
185 Willow Street
P.O. Box 180
Mystic, CT 06355
(860) 536-2611
(800) 321-0411
www.twentythirdpublications.com

ISBN 0-89622-938-6
Library of Congress Catalog Card Number 98-60916
Printed in the U.S.A.

Dedication

In Memory of Lois Darlene Vos (1942-1944), my sister, who died of leukemia before I was born. Although your death was a loss for family and friends, your life showed many people the love of God. (P.V.W.)

To my co-author and dearest friend, Phyllis Vos Wezeman, who has walked with me and remained my companion through many losses. For this I am full of gratitude. (J.D.F.)

To Fr. Ed Ruetz and Sr. Pauline Bridegroom, who have helped me and countless others live through a loss. (K.R.W.)

Contents

Guiding Children through Life's Losses

Introduction

Loss. To the baby it's a broken toy. To the second grader it's a misplaced lunch. To the ten year old it's a missing assignment. To the teenager it's a crashed hard drive. To the youth it's theft. To the young couple it's an accident. To the team it's defeat. To the parent it's unemployment. To the family it's moving to a new state. To the grandparent it's coping with the death of a spouse. To the town it's dealing with the effects of a flood.

Losses are minor; losses are major. Losses are expected; losses are unexpected. Losses are negative; losses are positive. Losses occur every day, from time to time, and throughout a lifetime. Losses happen to everyone, yet each person deals with loss—even the same loss—in a different way.

Guiding Children Through Life's Losses offers adults a way to help children deal with loss—losses that are anticipated, like changing grades or seasons; losses that are uncomfortable, like losing face or friends; and losses that are inevitable, like coping with disease or death. This resource develops sixteen themes to help young people acknowledge a loss, express feelings associated with the change, and recognize the experience as an opportunity for growth, all within the context of a prayer experience.

Each prayer service in this book is developed through a clear, creative, challenging, and ready-to-use format.

Explore states the purpose of the prayer service.

Emphasize highlights a Scripture text which illuminates the topic.

Exhibit recommends items to display on a prayer table.

Equipment lists required supplies and gives suggestions for advance preparation, where needed.

Explain provides an overview of the specific theme of loss.

Experience offers an outline for the prayer service, using several or all of the following elements:

• *Gathering song* sets the mood of the service. These suggestions can be adapted to suit your own music resources.

• *Gathering prayer or action* provides a welcoming gesture.

• *Reading* includes a Scripture passage or story.

• *Ritual* invites learners to explore the theme.

• *Response* offers a prayerful reaction to the ritual.

• *Closing prayer* and/or *closing song* concludes the prayer service.

Enhance presents three ways to enrich the experience.

Expand submits three ways to further develop the theme.

While the prayer services in *Guiding Children Through Life's Losses* are intended for young people in classroom settings, they may be easily adapted for use by older children, teenagers, and adults in small and large group worship, education, outreach, and nurture opportunities. They are ideal for parochial school programs, religious education classes, vacation Bible school courses, confirmation sessions, intergenerational events, youth groups, retreat settings, family devotions, home schooling, and more.

Guiding Children Through Life's Losses reminds leaders and participants to turn to God in every circumstance of life. Regardless of the losses that occur in our lives, God is always present to us and for us. Through prayer, we can spend time with God, pour out our hearts to God, and be assured of God's love—a love that survives any loss.

1
Divorce

EXPLORE

To provide an opportunity to explore the theme of divorce and to use activities to help children grow through the experience.

EMPHASIZE

God is our refuge and strength, a very present help in trouble.

—Psalm 46:1

EXHIBIT

- Basket of acorns
- Candle
- Paper oak leaves

EQUIPMENT

- Acorns
- Basket
- Bible(s)
- Bulletin board (optional)
- Butcher paper
- Candle
- Construction paper
- Covering for prayer table
- Markers
- Matches
- Music for "Hosea" (Monks of Weston Priory)
- Paint (optional)
- Paint brushes (optional)
- Pattern for oak leaf
- Patterns for oak tree trunk and branches
- Scissors
- Table
- Tacks or tape

Advance Preparation

🌰 Cut oak leaves from construction paper and spread them on the prayer table.

🌰 Cut the oak tree trunk and branches from butcher paper and color them with markers or paints. Prepare to hang the tree on a bulletin board or wall in the area where the service will be held or to pin the pieces to the front of the prayer cloth.

🌰 Fill a basket with acorns and place it on the prayer table.

🌰 Place supplies for the activity in the area where the prayer service will be held.

🌰 Set the candle and the matches on the prayer table.

EXPLAIN

Divorce is devastatingly disruptive to a family. It is not only a loss to a husband and wife, but to children, as well. First children have to face the fear of losing one of their parents—and then they have to face the reality of the separation. Often a child will think that he or she did something to cause the rift between the parents, especially if the parents have been arguing about how to raise the child(ren). The child may be unaware of many of the dynamics between the parents, but very aware of his or her misbehavior or shortcomings.

Children need to be reassured that they are loved and will receive the care they need. They also need the reassurance that God cares for them and will provide for their needs, protect them, and hold them in his loving arms. They also need to be reassured that the divorce is due to decisions of mom and/or dad and is no fault of theirs.

EXPERIENCE

Gathering Song

"Hosea"

Gathering Prayer

Leader: Loving and all compassionate God, we come to you as our Eternal Mother and Father. We pray that you will be with us and our earthly parents as we struggle to understand divorce. Guide us in love and com-

passion that our hearts may be healed from hurt and sadness. We ask this in the name of Jesus who is our constant friend. Amen.

Light the candle.

Reading

Invite one of the participants to read the story of Elzeard Bouffier, the man who planted trees.

He had planted 100,000 acorns; of these, 20,000 had come up; of these, he still expected to lose at least half either to rodents or to any of the other unpredictable things that only Providence can account for....

I never saw him lose heart...nor was he ever deterred and often, God knows, it must have seemed that heaven was against him. I never tried to imagine his frustration, but to achieve such an end he must have had to overcome many obstacles; for such passion to succeed he must have surely fought and conquered despair.

When I consider the passionate determination, the unfailing generosity of spirit it took to achieve this end, I am filled with admiration for this old man who was able to complete a task worthy of God. He was planting trees.
    —from *The Man Who Planted Trees*

Ritual

Many children have experienced divorce in their own families. Other children have friends or acquaintances who live in families where a mother or a father has left. Although mothers and fathers want what is best for their children, sometimes the caregivers cannot work together to accomplish this purpose. When this happens, and the mom and dad decide to divorce, it causes a variety of feelings: anger, frustration, guilt, loneliness, pain.

Show the students the basket of acorns on the prayer table. Remind them that acorns grow to become oak trees. Distribute one paper oak leaf to each participant. Talk to the children about how they are like acorns that are in the process of becoming oak trees. Sometimes the planting and growing process is hard and painful. Things happen that aren't expected. Many times the caregivers lose heart and leave. Sometimes they come back to continue nurturing what they planted; sometimes they don't. This doesn't mean that the caregivers no longer love the acorn, it only means they can't do the work together any more.

Distribute markers and ask each person to write a feeling related to divorce on their oak leaf. The feeling could be based on personal experience or on experiences shared with other people.

When each student has completed a leaf, begin constructing the bulletin board. First, hang up the large trunk

of the oak tree. Talk about how the trunk reminds us of God, our strength, the center of life. Next, place the branches on the tree as a reminder of the people who hold us up during difficult times, for example: friends, grandparents, moms, dads, teachers, aunts, uncles, pastors, people from church, and neighbors. Finally, invite the participants to come one at a time to place a leaf, writing side down, on the branches of the oak tree. After every three or four leaves are posted, ask the students to repeat the phrase: "Lord, help us grow strong in your name."

Closing Prayer

Leader: Psalm 46 reminds us that the God who made the acorn and the oak tree is our strength in life.

God is our refuge and strength,
an ever-present help in trouble.
Therefore we will not fear,
though the earth should change,
though the mountains shake
in the heart of the sea;
and the waters roar and foam.

There is a river whose streams make
glad the city of God,
the holy habitation
of the Most High.
God is in the midst of the city;
it shall not be moved;
God will help it
when the morning dawns.

The world is in an uproar,
the kingdoms totter;
God speaks and the earth melts.
The Lord of hosts is with us;
the God of Jacob is our refuge.

"Be still, and know that I am God!
I am exalted among the nations,
I am exalted in the earth."
The Lord of hosts is with us;
the God of Jacob is our refuge.

Leader: Ever mindful God, we know that you hear our every prayer. Thank you for walking with us in times of hurt and pain. You call us every day to trust you so that through Jesus we can grow strong in wisdom just as the acorn becomes the mighty oak. We pray this today because we believe. Amen.

As the prayer service concludes, give each student an acorn from the basket on the prayer table as a reminder that God will be with them as they continue to grow in love and faith.

ENHANCE

🌰 Make finger puppets from the acorns and use them to act out stories.

🌰 Read children's books about divorce as part of the service.

🌰 Set a branch in a container and invite the students to bring pictures to hang on the limbs to create a family tree.

EXPAND

🌰 Construct a paperweight or plaque containing an acorn, an oak leaf, and the passage from Psalm 46 cited in the "Emphasize" section.

🌰 Create a newspaper to help children deal with divorce. Assign the students topics such as "What I do on visits with my Mom," "Having two bedrooms," or "Here's how I handle anger." Instruct "reporters" to interview youth and adults and to write articles to include in the publication.

🌰 Obtain information about Rainbows for God's Children, a support group for children who have experienced separation and divorce.

2
Death of a Grandparent

EXPLORE

To use calendar journals to help students explore thoughts and feelings associated with the death of a grandparent.

EMPHASIZE

We do not want you to be uninformed, brothers and sisters, about those who have died, so that you may not grieve as others do who have no hope.
— 1 Thessalonians 4:13

EXHIBIT

- Bible(s)
- Candle
- Empty chair

EQUIPMENT

- Candle
- CD or tape player
- Chair
- Construction paper (12" x 18")
- Covering for prayer table
- Matches
- Music for "We Remember" (Marty Haugen) and "Happy Are They Who Believe" (David Haas)
- Pencils
- Photographs of grandparents (brought by participants)
- Rulers
- Table

Advance Preparation

❀ Invite the students to bring photos of grandparents who have died.

❀ Place supplies for the activity in the area where the prayer service will be held.

❀ Set the candle and matches on the prayer table and position the empty chair in front of the space.

EXPLAIN

For many children, the death of a grandparent is the first time they experience the loss of a significant person in their lives. Grandparents are often a source of unconditional love and acceptance. Children may have warm memories of ways in which they enjoyed this very special relationship. Eliciting those memories can be reassuring to children that this warmth and love can be carried with them in the future simply by recalling the past.

This may also be the first time for many children to hear the message that people who die in the Lord go to live with God. The death of a grandparent can then be used as a means to teach them the truth of the resurrection.

EXPERIENCE

Gathering Song

"We Remember"

Gathering Action

Invite each participant, in turn, to place a photograph of a grandparent on the empty chair and to share a memory of the person.

Light the candle.

Reading

But we do not want you to be uninformed, brothers and sisters, about those who have died, so that you may not grieve as others do who have no hope. For since we believe that Jesus died and rose again, even so, through Jesus, God will bring with him those who have died. Therefore encourage one another with these words.

—1 Thessalonians 4:13,14,18

Ritual

Even though death is a natural part of life, it is not easy to lose someone we love. Remark that the first year without a loved one can be a very difficult time. It is an important time to acknowledge thoughts and feelings related to the loss. For example, someone may feel sad because there is an empty place at the Christmas party; a child could be disappointed because he wasn't able to make grandma a special birthday card; and others could be angry because family traditions are changed.

Invite the group to make calendar journals to help them experience events following the death of a grandparent and to acknowledge their thoughts and feelings about this significant loss.

Distribute a 12" x 18" piece of construction paper to each participant. Offer pencils and rulers and instruct the students to measure and draw six equal squares on each side of the sheet. Next, tell the students to print the name of a month in a each space. If the month coincides with an event related to the grandmother or grandfather, the date and occasion should be written in the square. For example: January 25, grandpa's birthday, or May 17, grandma's birthday. Special holidays could be marked as well, such as Christmas, Easter, and Thanksgiving.

Tell the students to use the calendar journals to help them record thoughts and feelings about their grandparents as events occur each month. For example, "I missed grandma's cookies," might be written in the December square, or "I missed the fresh corn from grandpa's garden," could be recorded in the August block. The students in the group who have not had a grandparent die can do the same, but in the present tense: "I enjoy Grandma's cookies" in December, or in April, "Time for a walk with Grandpa!" Encourage the participants to decorate the calendars with drawings, photos, and mementos throughout the year.

Once the calendars are completed, invite the students to place them on the prayer table and to gather for the closing service.

Response

Leader: Come into our hearts, O God!

ALL: Come into our hearts, O God!

Leader: To guard us…

ALL: Come into our hearts, O God!

Leader: To strengthen us…

ALL: Come into our hearts, O God!

Leader: To find us…

ALL: Come into our hearts, O God!

Leader: To restore us…

ALL: Come into our hearts, O God!

Leader: To help us…

ALL: Come into our hearts, O God!

Leader: To delight us…

ALL: Come into our hearts, O God!

Leader: To change us…

ALL: Come into our hearts, O God!

Leader: To guide us…

ALL: Come into our hearts, O God!

Leader: To remember those we love who have died…

ALL: Come into our hearts, O God!

Closing Prayer

Leader: Ever loving God and giver of all good things, you sent your only son to gather all your children home into your loving arms; strengthen us in your holy name that we may praise you forever.

ALL: Amen.

Leader: Bow your heads and receive God's blessing… May God care for us as we await the fullness of life,

ALL: Amen.

Leader: May Jesus, our redemption, lead us gently home,

ALL: Amen.

Leader: May the Spirit breathe us into everlasting life,

ALL: Amen.

Closing Song

"Happy Are They Who Believe"

ENHANCE

✼ Decorate the prayer table with objects representing special days and holidays through the year.

✼ Invite parents of the students to share memories of their grandfathers and grandmothers.

✼ Light a candle representing each grandparent who has died.

EXPAND

✼ Create a family tree in an area of the classroom to celebrate the importance of grandparents, both those who are living and those who have died. Invite the students to bring photographs or to draw pictures of their grandparents and to attach them to a branch or bulletin board.

✼ Invite a speaker to share information about funerals.

✼ Visit a cemetery and, with permission, do rubbings of the gravestones.

3
Moving Away

EXPLORE

To offer prayer for God's guidance during a move to a new home.

EMPHASIZE

Remember, I am with you always, to the end of the age.
—Matthew 28:20

EXHIBIT

- Basket containing phrases of the litany
- Bushel basket of wooden blocks
- Empty bushel basket
- Map of new location or state
- Outline drawing of house
- Pillar candle
- Well-worn tennis shoes

EQUIPMENT

- Basket
- Bible(s)
- Bushel baskets (two)
- Copier
- Covering for prayer table
- Litany
- Map of new location or state
- Markers
- Matches

- Music for "Come And Journey With Me" (David Haas) and "On Eagle's Wings" (Michael Joncas)
- Newsprint or butcher paper
- Pattern for outline of house
- Pillar candle
- Scissors or paper cutter
- Tennis shoes (well-worn)
- Wooden blocks

Advance Preparation

🏠 Copy the litany, cut the phrases into strips, and place the pieces in a basket.

🏠 Prepare an outline drawing of a house and place it on the floor in front of the prayer table.

🏠 Spread a map over the prayer table and set a bushel basket of wooden blocks, plus the basket of litany phrases, a pillar candle, matches, and a pair of well-worn tennis shoes on top of it. Set an empty bushel basket in front of the table.

EXPLAIN

Moving involves multiple losses on many levels. Besides a change of a house or apartment, it may involve leaving friends, school, possibly extended family, familiar places, church, and so on. It may mean a radical change of environment like moving from the country to the city or the city to the suburbs. In any event it is a time of leaving the familiar, the known, the comfortable, where one knows one's place, for the unfamiliar, unknown, and uncomfortable, where one's place has yet to be discovered.

It is a comfort to know that God is everywhere. Just as God was with the people he loved in ancient times, God is with us today. Jesus said he would never leave us or forsake us. No matter where we may be, no matter what friends we may leave behind, Jesus, our best Friend, will be with us.

EXPERIENCE

Gathering Song:

"Come And Journey With Me"

Before the gathering song invite those gathered to remove their shoes and to place them in the empty bushel basket as a sign of trusting God in every move.

Gathering Prayer

Leader: Come and open our hearts.

ALL: Come and open our hearts.

Leader: We move to the guidance of God who is the Father,

ALL: Come and open our hearts.

Leader: We move to the love of God who is the Son,

ALL: Come and open our hearts.

Leader: We move through the power of God who is the Spirit,

ALL: Come and open our hearts.

Leader: God, who is Father, Son and Spirit, we know that simply being in your holy presence is communal prayer. Our every joy, our every sorrow, our every desire, our every move made in your presence is prayer. Give us courage and a sense of adventure, Guiding God, as we begin a journey to a new place and a new experience. Amen.

Light the candle.

Reading

Then Peter said, "Look, we have left our homes and followed you." And he said to them, "Truly I tell you, there is no one who has left house or wife or brothers or parents or children, for the sake of the kingdom of God, who will not get back very much more in this age, and in the age to come eternal life."

—Luke 18:28–30

Ritual

Explain that (Name) is moving to (Place). Invite the group to participate in a responsive prayer asking for God's guidance during this move. Ask each participant to select a wooden block from the bushel basket and to pick a slip of paper from the container with the lines of the litany.

Gather the group around the edges of the outline of the house. Prepare the group for prayer by directing the students to take turns reading one line of the litany, then placing a block on the outline.

Guide one student at a time to read a line of the prayer and to place a block on the outline. Invite the group to repeat the response together.

Litany

Leader: After each phrase of the litany, please respond with the words "Be with us (or use Name) in this move."

Jesus you are Light for the way...

ALL: Be with us in this move.

Jesus you guide all who are lost.

(Continue with "All" response after each prayer, as above.)

Jesus you are the Spirit that moves us.

Jesus you are the hand that leads us.

Jesus you are the bright star in the night sky.

Jesus you are the order in our chaos.

Jesus you are the one who shows us the way.

Jesus you have been with us throughout time.

Jesus we enjoy your presence.

Jesus you are brightness where there is obscurity.

Jesus you are warmth when the journey is harsh.

Jesus you are the laughter where there is pain.

Jesus you are the purpose in our confusion.

Jesus you walk with us in all we do.

Jesus we make our home in you.

Jesus you are the beginning and the end.

Jesus you said, "I will be with you always, even until the end of the world."

Leader: May our every move be in the name of God, our faithful Creator, our loving Savior, and our guiding Spirit. Amen.

Closing Song

"On Eagle's Wings"

Before playing or singing the music, direct the participants, in turn, to go to the bushel basket to find their shoes and to return to the circle to put them on their feet. Suggest a time of silent prayer reflecting on God's guidance in all of life's moves.

ENHANCE

🏠 Invite the students to share their experiences of moving.

🏠 Place pushpins on a map of the United States (or the world) to indicate places where the students have lived.

🏠 Using a map of Bible times, trace the journeys of the Israelites or of one particular person such as the Apostle Paul.

EXPAND

🏠 Construct models of homes ranging from chalets to cliff dwellings, tepees to tents, and houseboats to haciendas! Refer to the book *People*, by Peter Spier (Garden City, NY: Doubleday, 1980) for illustrations of twenty-five types of homes found throughout the world.

🏠 Contact a moving company to obtain "moving kits" for children.

🏠 Create "Welcome" mats, signs, or wreaths to give to new families that move to the school or parish.

4
Death of a Classmate

EXPLORE

To prayerfully reflect on the life of a classmate who has died and to create a scrapbook of memories celebrating the life of the person.

EMPHASIZE

Then the Lord God will wipe away the tears from all faces.

—Isaiah 25:8

EXHIBIT

- Candle
- Empty scrapbook

EQUIPMENT

- Bible(s)
- Candle
- CD or tape player
- Construction paper (white)
- Covering for prayer table
- Crayons
- Glue sticks
- Markers
- Matches
- Music for "You Are Mine" (David Haas)
- Pencils
- Photo tabs (optional)
- Scrapbook
- Table

Advance Preparation

✸ Place supplies for the scrapbook-making activity in the area where the prayer service will be held.

✸ Set the candle, matches, and empty scrapbook on the prayer table.

EXPLAIN

The death of a classmate or friend is often the first time a child is confronted with the fact that he or she is mortal. Grandparents, uncles and aunts, even parents may die, yet because they are so much older, children may not fully experience their loss as an indication of their own mortality. In the loss of a classmate, children encounter the fact that life may be brief; in fact, much more brief than they ever thought possible.

Another issue may also face children who lose a classmate. Children, being human, often hurt each other by words or actions. Surviving children are often burdened by guilt because they never said they were sorry or never had the opportunity to make amends. Children need the opportunity to be forgiven for the hurt they may have caused another, as well to celebrate the life of someone they loved.

EXPERIENCE

Gathering Song
"You Are Mine"

Gathering Prayer
O God of beginnings and God of endings, we pause for a moment to remember our friend and classmate (Name) who has died. We ask you, Compassionate God, to give us the courage to celebrate the life of our friend with a joyful heart. We know that Jesus, who died for all people, has taken away the sting of death. Be with us now and always as we find strength in the love of Christ. Amen.

Light the candle.

Reading
It was late Saturday morning by the time I got to Tommy's house. We played together every Saturday. Tommy's my best friend. We attend the same school and have the same teacher, Mrs. Martin. Summer vacation will be here soon and then we'll play together every day. We will fish in the pond, hike in the woods, climb trees in the orchard, play hide-and-go-seek in the barn, and laugh a lot. Tommy and I have fun together. But this Saturday everything was different.

On Wednesday Mrs. Martin told us that Tommy was very sick and that we needed to pray for him. I knew by Saturday Tommy would be better.

On Saturday Tommy's father came outside instead of Tommy. He said he wanted to talk to me. We sat on the grass; it was warm outside. He told me that Tommy was sick, very sick. Tommy's father took my hand and told me that Tommy was not going to get better; Tommy was going to die.

On Monday Mrs. Martin told us that Tommy would not be coming back to school. A doctor came to talk to us about Tommy's illness and to answer our questions. He told us that even though Tommy was sick we could still be his friends. He told us we could visit Tommy, eat with him, and even give Tommy hugs. The doctor told us we should not be afraid of Tommy. I'm not; Tommy's my best friend.

I saw Tommy when he came home from the hospital. It was good to see him. He didn't look much like Tommy. He was real skinny. But I knew it was Tommy; he always made me laugh. We ate soup and crackers and chocolate pudding. It was real good. Tommy couldn't eat much of his. His mom and dad tried to feed him. Tommy's mom and dad are very sad. It hurts them to see Tommy so sick. They hold hands and hug a lot and Tommy doesn't mind. I even see them cry. I cry too.

Tommy stayed in bed the last few days. He liked it when I read to him. I didn't wait until Saturday; I visited him every day. When Tommy died it made me very sad. I will miss him very much. I loved him. He was my best friend.

Ritual

Allow time for the participants to respond to the story. Let the students express their feelings about Tommy's death and his friend's love and care. Encourage the listeners to talk about the death of their friend or classmate. Allow time for the students to share memories and to express emotions.

Hold up a scrapbook and ask someone to explain its purpose. Ask people who have made scrapbooks to raise their hands. Invite the group to name some of the things they have put in their scrapbooks. Tell the students that they will make a scrapbook to celebrate the life of (Name).

Direct the students to recall memories of (Name). Suggest experiences in and out of the classroom. Offer each participant a piece of construction paper, crayons, markers, and pencils, and guide the group as they create their pictures. Once the drawings are completed, ask the children to write a brief note on the back of the paper. The note could be about the picture or it could be a statement to the friend.

Dim the lights and ask the students to sit in silence remembering their classmate. Encourage them to say a silent prayer of thanks for the life of (Name). Play the song "You Are Mine" and invite the participants to come, one at a time, to glue their drawing into the scrapbook.

Response

On this mountain the Lord of hosts will make for all peoples a feast of rich food, a feast of well-aged wines, of rich food filled with marrow, of well-aged wines strained clear. And he will destroy on this mountain the shroud that is cast over all peoples, the sheet that is spread over all nations; he will swallow up death forever. Then the Lord God will wipe away the tears from all faces, and the disgrace of his people he will take away from all the earth, for the Lord has spoken.

—Isaiah 25:6–8

Invite everyone to join hands and pray the Lord's Prayer.

ENHANCE

❁ Create a bulletin board or a photo collage celebrating the life of the deceased.

❁ If appropriate, invite the family of the classmate to attend the prayer service.

❁ Read the story of Jesus' resurrection in Matthew 28:1–10, Mark 16:1–8, Luke 24:1–12, or John 20:1–10.

EXPAND

❁ Arrange for a pastor to talk with the group about memorial services that celebrate the life of someone who has died.

❁ Invite a counselor to speak to the group about death.

❁ Set up an area in the classroom with children's books on the theme of death.

5

An Accident

EXPLORE

To pray for someone involved in an accident and to use "binding" cloths to symbolize Jesus' healing mercy.

EMPHASIZE

He will feed his flock like a shepherd; he will gather the lambs in his arms, and carry them in his bosom, and gently lead the mother sheep.

—Isaiah 40:11

EXHIBIT

- Basket of white fabric strips
- Candle

EQUIPMENT

- Basket
- Bible(s)
- Candle
- CD or tape player
- Covering for prayer table
- Matches
- Music for "Healing Hands" (Elton John), "On Eagle's Wings" (Michael Joncas), or "He Shall Feed His Flock" from Handel's *Messiah*.

- Permanent markers
- Scissors

- Table
- White fabric

Advance Preparation

🍃 Cut white fabric into strips and place the pieces in a basket.

🍃 Place supplies for the activity in the area where the prayer service will be held.

🍃 Set the basket of white fabric strips, candle, and matches on the prayer table.

🍃 Make copies of the gathering prayer to give to readers.

EXPLAIN

Accidents involve losses on many levels. They may entail loss of time, money, possessions, opportunity, mobility, and so forth. They intrude upon our lives suddenly and unexpectedly, often causing pain and suffering.

Nothing forces us to face mortality as much as a sudden serious accident. We are abruptly reminded of the fact that we are not here permanently, and this can cause us intense pain. Or if the accident happens to someone we love, we are reminded that our time together may be much more brief than we expected.

When an accident occurs we often come together with family and friends and find comfort in their presence. We are comforted because they are still there, still with us. Whatever loss we may have experienced, we still have those we love. As believers, we also find comfort in the fact that the Lord is with us. Even though we may be like grass, as Isaiah tells the people in the prayer we will read below, God is always with us, holding us in the palm of his hand.

EXPERIENCE

Gathering Song

"Healing Hands," "On Eagle's Wings," or "He Shall Feed His Flock"

Play a recording of one of these songs softly during the gathering prayer.

Gathering Prayer

Leader: Listen to God's Word from the prophet Isaiah (40:6–11, 29, 31): A voice says, "Cry out!" And I said, "What shall I cry?" All people are grass, their constancy is like the flower of the field.

Reader One: The grass withers, the flower fades, when the breath of the Lord blows upon it; surely the people are grass.

ALL: The grass withers, the flower fades; but the word of our God will stand forever.

Leader: Get you up to a high mountain, O Zion, herald of good tidings; lift up your voice with strength, O Jerusalem, herald of good tidings, lift it up, do not fear; say to the cities of Judah, "Here is your God!"

Reader Two: See, the Lord God comes with might, and his arm rules for him; his reward is with him, and his recompense before him.

Leader: He will feed his flock like a shepherd; he will gather the lambs in his arms, and carry them in his bosom, and gently lead the mother sheep.

Reader Three: He gives power to the faint, and strengthens the powerless.

Leader: Those who wait for the Lord shall renew their strength, they shall mount up with wings like eagles, they shall run and not be weary, they shall walk and not faint.

Light the candle.

Reading

Have an adult or child read John 11:17–44 from the Bible or a children's lectionary.

Before the reading, invite six participants to come forward. Use six strips of white cloth from the basket and bind each person's hands in a "praying hands" position. Direct the six students to stand facing the group.

Begin the reading. When it is finished, the reader should unbind the hands of one of the six students and instruct that person to unbind the hands of the next person, and so on. The six should then take the basket of fabric strips from the prayer table and distribute one piece to each participant.

Ritual

Talk to the participants about the day-to-day accidents and injuries that occur in a person's life. Cite examples such as broken arms or legs, injuries to feet or hands, cuts and bruises, major or minor burns, car collisions or sporting mishaps. Allow the students time to share personal experiences of accidents or injuries.

Move from this discussion to remind the group of ways that Jesus binds our wounds. Explain that God provides people to help us through accidents and injuries, for example, moms, dads, grandparents, doctors, nurses, teachers, friends, and others. Jesus promises to take care of his people like a shepherd cares for his sheep.

Pass out the markers and invite the children to write, on one side of their cloth, a time when they were injured in some way. Examples could include: broke my arm playing hockey, sprained my ankle during soccer, or crashed my bike and hurt my wrist. Next direct the group to turn their strips over and to write at least one way that someone helped them through the experience. For example,

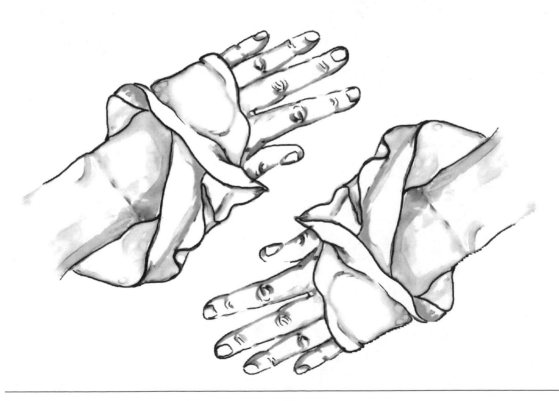

a neighbor put my bike in his car and took me home, or the coach taped my ankle. In small groups allow the participants time to share their responses.

Response

Gather the students in a circle around the prayer table. Invite the participants to tie their binding cloths together one at a time, not letting go of their end. Pray the following words while this is taking place.

Leader: Lord, come and heal us.

ALL: Lord, come and heal us.

Leader: For all those who are hurt because of accidents, we pray…

ALL: Lord, come and heal us.

Leader: For all people who have been physically hurt in any way, that they may find healing in Jesus, we pray…

ALL: Lord, come and heal us.

Leader: For all those in our family or class who are suffering bodily pain, that they may find comfort in Jesus' care, we pray…

ALL: Lord, come and heal us.

Leader: For those who hurt and harm others, that they may have a change of heart through the power of God's love, we pray…

ALL: Lord, come and heal us.

Leader: For the poor who live in all parts of the world, that all nations will work to bring about peace and justice so as to alleviate hurt and pain, we pray…

ALL: Lord, come and heal us.

Leader: That we may use our hands for healing and not for hurting, we pray…

ALL: Lord, come and heal us. Amen.

Once all of the binding cloths are tied together, continue holding the cloth and together pray the Lord's Prayer.

Closing Song

Repeat the Gathering Song or choose another song from that list.

ENHANCE

🌿 Create a mural depicting the Lazarus story and highlight the pictures as the Scripture passage is read.

🌿 Erect a three-dimensional display of medical supplies such as bandages and crutches in the prayer space.

🌿 Place a "Praying Hands" symbol on the prayer table.

EXPAND

🌿 Arrange to tour a hospital emergency room and to have the medical staff speak about treatment of people who have been involved in accidents.

🌿 Review New Testament stories of Jesus' healing ministry.

🌿 Teach basic first aid methods.

6

Terminal Illness

Explore

To explore emotions associated with serious illness and to learn ways to acknowledge and express these feelings.

Emphasize

Come to me, all you that are weary and are carrying heavy burdens, and I will give you rest.

—Matthew 11:28

Exhibit

- Candle
- Diary (blank)

Equipment

- Bible(s)
- Candle
- CD or tape player
- Covering for prayer table
- Diary (blank)
- Index cards
- Matches
- Music for "Isaiah 49" (Carey Landry) or "Every Heartbeat" (Amy Grant)
- Pens
- Table

- Tape (cellophane)

Advance Preparation

♡ Place supplies for the activity in the area where the prayer service will be held.

♡ Set the candle, diary, and matches on the prayer table.

♡ Write "I feel…" on one or two index cards for each participant.

Explain

A person experiencing a terminal illness is anticipating a very great loss, the loss of his or her own life. Friends and family of a person with terminal illness face the loss of someone they love. There are also many other losses along the way including the loss of independence, friends, income, and health. Facing all these losses stirs up many emotions.

Dr. Elisabeth Kübler-Ross identified these emotional states with stages of grieving: denial, depression, anger, bargaining, and acceptance. These emotions are really common to all types of loss, but stand out more dramatically when facing death. They are very normal and very human.

Jesus went through the same kinds of emotions that face us. He wept over the loss of his friend Lazarus. He went off to grieve after the death of his cousin, John the Baptist. Jesus was sad as he faced his own death, yet he finally accepted the fact that he must die so that we could have eternal life. We can be assured as we face our death, or the death of someone important to us, that Jesus understands what it is like, and that he will be there to support and comfort us.

EXPERIENCE

Gathering Song

"Isaiah 49" or "Every Heartbeat"

Gathering Prayer

Leader: God of every emotion, we come to you to share our feelings. We gather to pray for (Name) who is seriously ill. Give us the courage to place our concerns in your hands. We ask this in the name of Jesus, our compassionate friend, who died to give us life. Amen.

Light the candle.

Readings

Invite two students to each read one of the following Scripture passages.

When Martha heard that Jesus was coming, she went and met him, while Mary stayed at home. Martha said to Jesus, "Lord, if you had been here, my

brother would not have died. But even now I know that God will give you whatever you ask of him."

When Jesus saw her weeping, and the Jews who came with her also weeping, he was greatly disturbed in spirit and deeply moved. He said, "Where have you laid him?" They said to him, "Lord, come and see." Jesus began to weep.
—John 11:20–22, 33–35

Pause.

Then Jesus went with them to a place called Gethsemane; and he said to his disciples, "Sit here while I go over there and pray." He took with him Peter and the two sons of Zebedee, and began to be grieved and agitated. Then he said to them, "I am deeply grieved, even to death; remain here, and stay awake with me." And going a little farther, he threw himself on the ground and prayed, "My Father, if it is possible, let this cup pass from me; yet not what I want but what you want."

Then he came to the disciples and found them sleeping; and he said to Peter, "So, could you not stay awake with me one hour? Stay awake and pray that you may not come into the time of trial; the spirit indeed is willing, but the flesh is weak."

Again he went away for the second time and prayed, "My Father, if this cannot pass unless I drink it, your will be done." Again he came and found them sleeping, for their eyes were heavy. So leaving them again, he went away and prayed for the third time, saying the same words. Then he came to the disciples and said to them, "Are you still sleeping and taking your rest?

See, the hour is at hand, and the Son of Man is betrayed into the hands of sinners. Get up, let us be going. See, my betrayer is at hand."

—Matthew 26:36–46

Pause.

Ritual

After the readings invite the young people to reflect on the variety of emotions expressed in the Bible passages. Take time to name or list some of the feelings suggested in the Scripture stories. Jesus felt sad when Lazarus died. Jesus was troubled when he prayed in the Garden of Gethsemane and disappointed when the disciples fell asleep as they waited for him. Even though Jesus was divine, he was also human and experienced a variety of emotions during his life on earth.

Explain that feelings are a natural part of life, yet they are often difficult to express and hard to understand. Tell the group that people who are seriously ill, as well as their families and friends, experience a variety of emotions. When we think about the serious illness of (Name) we experience a variety of feelings, too. Each person will have the opportunity to name and describe an emotion that they experience as they think about (Name)'s illness. Show an example of an "I feel…" card. Provide examples such as "I feel sad that (Name) won't be on the team," "I feel sorry for (Name)'s family," or "I feel thankful that (Name) was in my class." Assure the group that all feelings are acceptable; there are no right or wrong responses. Each person reacts to serious illness in a personal way. Tell the group that they will tape their cards to the blank pages of the diary on the prayer table; they will not be asked to share their feelings with the entire group.

Distribute the cards and pens and guide the group as they complete the sentences. Remind the pupils that they are to name an emotion and to write a phrase describing this feeling.

After the cards are completed, invite the participants to come forward, one at a time, to tape the card to a blank page of the diary. Play tranquil music as the ritual takes place.

Closing Reading

Leader: Listen to the words of Jesus, our caring Savior:

> *Come to me, all you that are weary and are carrying heavy burdens, and I will give you rest. Take my yoke upon you, and learn from me; for I am gentle and humble in heart, and you will find rest for your souls. For my yoke is easy, and my burden is light.*
> —Matthew 11:28–30

ENHANCE

♡ Arrange for a number of adults to be present during the service to talk about feelings with the participants individually or in small groups.

♡ Invite the students to remember (Name) in prayer every day.

♡ Provide additional supplies and ask each person to add a page to the diary naming a special gift—such as friendship, kindness, or laughter— that they received from (Name).

EXPAND

♡ Acquaint the participants with local and national groups that help critically ill children and their families such as:

Make A Wish Foundation
1600 N. Central Avenue, Suite 936
Phoenix, AZ 85004
(602) 240-6600

Ronald McDonald House
McDonald's Corporation
Kroc Drive
Oakbrook, IL 60521
(708) 575-7418

♡ Invite a speaker from an organization such as Hospice to share with the group.

♡ Provide an opportunity for the students to remember the family of the critically ill person with a card, a plate of cookies, or another act of kindness.

7
Parent's Loss of a Job

EXPLORE

To offer prayer support for persons involved in situations of unemployment.

EMPHASIZE

Jesus said to them, "I am the bread of life. Whoever comes to me will never be hungry, and whoever believes in me will never be thirsty."

—John 6:35

EXHIBIT

- Candle
- Loaf of bread

EQUIPMENT

- Bible(s)
- Candle
- CD or tape player
- Covering for prayer table
- Loaf of bread
- Matches
- Music for "Amazing Grace" and "Taste and See" (Bob Hurd)
- Paper
- Pencils or pens
- Table

Advance Preparation

🍓 Place supplies for the activity in the area where the prayer service will be held.

🍓 Set the bread, candle, and matches on the prayer table.

EXPLAIN

When a parent loses a job, it may involve many losses. In addition to the work itself and loss of income, there may be losses in entertainment, life-style, time, self-esteem, possessions, and pastimes.

Many of us confuse our wants and our needs. Our wants may be many, but our actual needs are few. We need shelter, food, and clothing, but we may want many other things—or we may want specific kinds of shelter, food, and clothing. A time of unemployment may actually draw some families closer together, but this may be of small consolation to a child who is experiencing loss. Sometimes a simple sharing of bread in the right context may bring an assurance that others are concerned and that our needs will be met—by a loving God who will supply our daily bread as well as the bread of life.

EXPERIENCE

Gathering Song

"Amazing Grace"

Gathering Prayer

God, thank you for Jesus, the bread from heaven that gives life to the world. Amen.

Light the candle.

Reading

Jesus said to them, "Suppose one of you has a friend, and you go to him at midnight and say to him, 'Friend, lend me three loaves of bread; for a friend of mine has arrived, and I have nothing to set before him.' And he answers from within, 'Do not bother me; the door has already been locked, and my children are with me in bed; I cannot get up and give you anything.' I tell you, even though he will not get up and give him anything because he is his friend, at least because of his persistence he will get up and give him whatever he needs.

"So I say to you, Ask, and it will be given you; search, and you will find; knock, and the door will be opened for you."

—Luke 11:5–10

Reading

Share the following story about unemployment.

Michael walked into the kitchen for an after school snack. His grandma was busy preparing the evening meal. "I like having you here, Grandma, but I sure miss seeing Mom when I get home from school," he remarked.

Michael sat at the table and watched his grandma take a loaf of fresh bread from the oven. He always liked having his grandma visit, but this was more than a visit. She was helping out while his Mom worked extra hours and his Dad looked for a new job.

"We will keep praying that your dad finds a new job soon so your mother doesn't have to work late anymore," Michael's grandmother replied.

"Grandma, why did Dad lose his job?" Michael asked.

"Well, dear," explained Grandma, "businesses and factories lay people off for reasons like saving money, decreasing work, or changing technology. There are many people who are unemployed. I know your Dad will find work in the future, but it might take awhile. Until then, some things just have to change."

A lot had already changed, more than just having his grandma help out and his mom work more hours. Michael missed buying pizza every Friday night and spending money on movies every Saturday. He missed special snacks from the grocery store and he was sure he wouldn't get a bike for his birthday. Michael had extra jobs to do around the house and he spent more time taking care of his little sister. She was fun alright, but it meant he had less time to spend with his own friends.

There were other changes, too, but they weren't too bad: fresh home-baked bread, new books and videos from the library, and fun family games almost every night. Mom was planning a picnic for Saturday and Dad said Michael could plant a garden in the spring.

"Michael, would you like to be the first to try my famous raisin bread," Grandma asked. "It's better than store-bought bread any day," she added proudly as she handed him a thick slice.

Michael took a big bite. "I guess there are some things that money can't buy," he said with a smile.

Ritual

Unemployment means that someone is without a paying job. When a parent or a caregiver loses his or her job, change takes place in the family. Remind the class of the story about Michael's family. Ask volunteers to name some of the changes that took place when his Dad lost his job. Answers might include his Mom worked longer hours, Michael had to do more tasks, and he had to give up special treats.

When changes occur due to unemployment, choices have to be made. Sometimes people have to learn to separate needs from wants. Explain the difference between needs and

wants. Everyone needs food, but some people want it from an expensive restaurant. People might want to see a movie, but they don't need to see it at the most expensive showing. Young people need shoes, and they might want a certain brand, but they probably don't need it.

Distribute paper and pencils or pens to the group. Direct the participants to fold the paper in half to form two sides. Instruct them to print the words "Things I need" on the top of the left side and to letter the phrase "Things I want" on the top of the right half. Challenge each person to list ten items in each column. Invite volunteers to share their responses.

Closing Prayer

Direct the group's attention to the loaf of bread on the prayer table. Explain that bread is a common and simple food staple for people around the world. Bread also reminds us that God sent Jesus, the Bread of Life, to fill our needs—physical, emotional, and spiritual.

Invite the students to offer prayers of thanks that God provides for their needs. Statements could include thanks for families, for houses, and for food. As a response to each phrase the group could repeat the words "We give thanks to you, our God."

At the end of the litany, break the bread and share it with the children.

Closing Song
"Taste and See"

ENHANCE

🍓 Display a variety of types of bread on the prayer table.

🍓 Read bread-related stories in the Bible including Exodus 12:17–20 (the Passover); Exodus 16:4–5, 13–34 (manna in the wilderness); Matthew 26:26 (the Lord's Supper); and Luke 24:30–35 (the Emmaus story).

🍓 Share a story and activity based on the hymn "Guide Me, O Thou Great Jehovah" from the book *Hymn Stories For Children: Resources For Children's Worship* (Wezeman, Phyllis Vos and Anna L. Liechty, Grand Rapids, MI: Kregel Publications, 1995).

EXPAND

🍓 Bake bread and share it with people in the congregation or in the neighborhood or hold a bread sale and donate the profits to a specific cause.

🍓 Role play a family meeting to model a way to discuss finances.

🍓 Start a "job jar." Print daily jobs on separate slips of paper and place them in a large jar. Invite each person to pick one a day and to be responsible for completing the task.

8
Floods and Natural Disasters

EXPLORE

To review the story of Noah and to construct rainbow banners for use during a prayer time for people affected by floods and other natural disasters.

EMPHASIZE

"I establish my covenant with you, that never again shall all flesh be cut off by the waters of a flood, and never again shall there be a flood to destroy the earth." God said, "This is the sign of the covenant that I make between me and you and every living creature that is with you, for all future generations: I have set my bow in the clouds, and it shall be a sign of the covenant between me and the earth."

—Genesis 9:11–13

EXHIBIT

- Bowl of water
- Rainbow candle

EQUIPMENT

- Bible(s)
- Bowl
- CD or tape player
- Cord or yarn
- Dowel rods
- Glue
- Matches
- Music for "Come to the Water" (John Foley)
- Rainbow candle
- Ribbon, 1" wide (violet, indigo, blue, green, yellow, orange, red)
- Saw
- Scissors
- Table
- Water

Advance Preparation

※ Cut dowel rods into 8"–10" lengths.

※ Cut ribbon into 12" lengths. One piece of each color is needed for each participant.

※ Place rainbow banner supplies in the area where the prayer service will be held.

❋ Set a bowl of water, a rainbow candle, and matches on the prayer table.

EXPLAIN

Floods can be devastating for a community. Each year more than 300,000 people are driven from their homes and 200 people are killed by floods in the United States alone. Economic losses are also devastating. The floods caused by Hurricane Agnes, for example, resulted in $4.7 billion in damage. While some floods come slowly, giving communities time to evacuate, flash floods can strike suddenly and without warning, carrying away everything and everyone in their path.

Floods are devastating for families and individuals as well. They ravage homes and possessions. Family keepsakes, pictures, and heirlooms may be ruined. This destroys not only property, but also ties with the past and family history.

The same water that brings devastation brings life to thirsty people and a thirsty land. Water is sometimes devastating, but it is more often life-giving. The rainbow is a symbol of God's promise to never again destroy the world by flood. Rainbows require water droplets. The water that makes the rainbow happen is a different form of the same substance that brought destruction. God transforms the symbol of death into a symbol of life.

EXPERIENCE

Gathering Song
"Come to the Water"

Gathering Prayer

Leader: God of all the earth, come to our assistance.

ALL: God of all the earth, make haste to help us.

Leader: Let justice flow like water, and compassion like an unfailing river.

ALL: God of all the earth, make haste to help us.

Leader: Rise, gentle, yet powerful God, raise your hand, do not forget those who are in need; most especially the people in (flood location).

ALL: God of all the earth, make haste to help us.

Leader: You, God, see the distress and grief that affect your people; take them into your care.

ALL: God of all the earth, make haste to help us.

Leader: Gentle Creator, you know the wants of all your creation. Bring strength to the hearts of these people. Grant them a new day, with a sign of your rainbow promise.

ALL: God of all the earth, make haste to help us. Amen.

Light the rainbow candle.

Reading

Invite four people to each read a paragraph of this story, based on Genesis, chapters 8 and 9.

Reader One: At first light, Noah lifted the hatch and looked out. In fact, the whole family wanted to peep, all at the same time. The fresh air was delicious! All around there was nothing but dark water and gray clouds. There was certainly no sign of land.

Noah fetched a dove. He released it and watched it fly away. "If the dove returns," he said, "we'll know there's not a dry spot out there for the bird to land." Sure enough, the dove returned at nightfall. She was nearly exhausted, and hadn't found a tree or a rocky ledge in all her travels. The land was still covered with water.

Noah stretched out his hand and brought the bird inside.

Reader Two: A week later, Noah released the dove again. They saw nothing of her all day. And then, in the evening, she came swooping down and landed by the hatch. She had something in her beak.

Noah looked closely. The dove was carrying a fresh olive branch! It had found a tree top, so the flood waters must be going down. Everyone began to talk at once. Meanwhile, the dove sat, looking puzzled All she wanted to do was to build a nest, but she couldn't do much with only one twig.

Reader Three: Noah waited another seven days. Once again he set the dove free and this time she did not return. Early the next morning Noah slowly opened the hatch of the ark and stood on the deck with his wife. They blinked at the light of the rising sun. Soon, they were joined by the rest of their family. "Mud," said one of Noah's sons. "Nothing but mud." "But it's land, and the mud will soon be dry," said another. "And we are all still alive!" Noah and his family built an altar and gave thanks to God.

Reader Four: High over their heads arched a rainbow. They looked at it in wonder. It was every color under the sun and perfectly formed. As they gazed up into the sky, the Lord spoke: "I promise every living creature that the earth and those living on it will never again be destroyed by a flood. The rainbow that I have put in the sky will be my sign to you and to every living creature on earth. It will remind you that I will keep this promise forever."

Ritual

Floods have occurred since the beginning of time, and floods still occur today. Floods can happen anywhere; they can be anticipated or sudden. Many times people in floods lose their homes and their possessions; sometimes they even lose their lives. God provides for people, even in the midst of floods. One way God provides for people involved in floods is by having other people remember them in prayer.

Invite the students to remember the people of (flood location) by making rainbow banners, writing petitions on the ribbons, and offering their prayers to God. Explain that each person will make a banner containing one strip of ribbon for each color of the rainbow. A prayer for people experiencing floods will be written on each piece. Once the strips are completed, they will be attached to a dowel rod, side-by-side, in rainbow order: violet, indigo, blue, green, yellow, orange, and red.

Offer suggestions for prayer petitions such as "God, be with the people who have lost their homes;" "Be with those who are scared;" "Comfort those who have lost a pet;" "Thank you, God, for people who are bringing food;" "Thank you for your rainbow promise."

Distribute ribbon strips and permanent markers and guide the group as they print their prayers on the pieces. Once the writing is completed, help each participant glue his or her ribbons to the top of a dowel rod. Attach a piece of cord or yarn to each end of the dowel rod to form a hanger. Display the banners on a wall or table.

Response

As a prayer litany, invite the participants to read the petitions from their rainbow banners. After each person's turn, invite the group to respond with the words: "Lord, hear our prayer."

Closing Prayer and Song

Play "Come to the Water" again and invite the listeners to come to the basin and dip their fingers in. Remind the group of water's life-giving qualities as well as its destructive powers.

ENHANCE

※ Cover the prayer table with rainbow fabric.

※ Hold the prayer service at a body of water.

※ Show a news report or a video clip about a flood.

EXPAND

※ Contact the American Red Cross for information about flood relief.

※ Make and use puppets to act out the story of Noah and the Flood.

※ Refer to the "I Was Thirsty" chapter of the book *When Did We See You* (Wezeman, Phyllis Vos and Colleen Aalsburg Wiessner. Notre Dame, IN: Ave Maria Press, 1994) for additional water-themed activities.

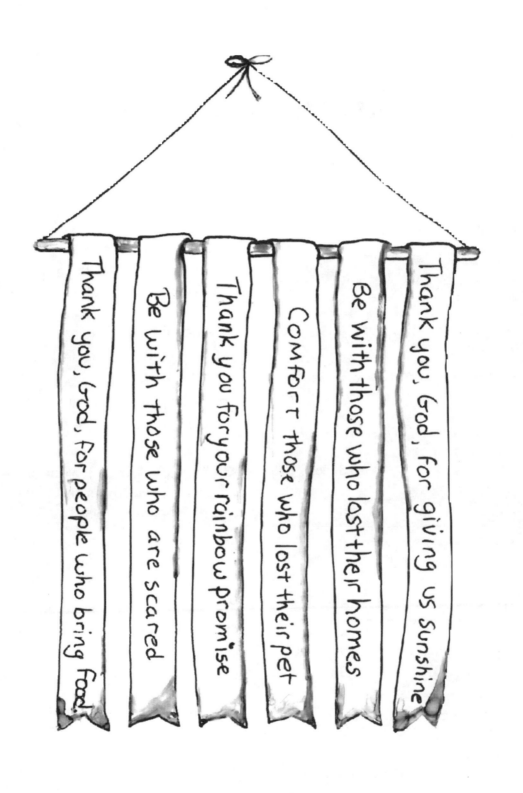

Thank you, God, for people who bring food

Be with those who are scared

Thank you for your rainbow promise

Comfort those who lost their pet

Be with those who lost their homes

Thank you, God, for giving us sunshine

9
Losing a Pet

EXPLORE

To pray for the safe return of a lost pet and to acknowledge the special relationship between a child and a pet.

EMPHASIZE

God made the wild animals of the earth of every kind, and the cattle of every kind, and everything that creeps upon the ground of every kind. And God saw that it was good.

—Genesis 1:25

EXHIBIT

- Candle
- Photograph of the lost pet

EQUIPMENT

- Basket
- Bible(s)
- Candle
- CD or tape player
- Covering for prayer table
- Markers
- Matches
- Music for "All Creatures of Our God and King," "All Things Bright and Beautiful," or "Morning Has Broken"
- Paper
- Photographs of pets
- Photograph of the lost pet
- Table

Advance Preparation

☞ Invite the students to bring photographs of pets.

☞ Obtain a photograph or sketch of the lost pet and place it on the prayer table.

☞ Type out words for one or two of the song selections and make copies for participants.

☞ Place supplies for the activity in the area where the prayer service will be held.

☞ Set the candles and matches on the prayer table.

EXPLAIN

A pet can be a very important member of the family. It may be there to greet you when you come home. It may be a companion with which you have spent many happy hours. The loss of a pet is a minor matter only to those who have not had such a relationship.

A missing pet may be more disturbing than a pet that has died. A child may wonder if he or she was careless in not watching the pet more carefully. Another child may be preoccupied by the anxiety that goes with wondering if the pet will return and may be distracted by every bark or meow that is heard. A missing pet can disrupt a life with anxiety and grief.

Children can be assured that the loving Creator that made all living things cares for them and their pets. Jesus said that God cares for the sparrow, and he cares for us and our pets. God made the animals and they are important to him. Regardless of what may happen, our animals are in God's hands, just as we are.

EXPERIENCE

Gathering Song

"All Creatures of Our God and King," "All Things Bright and Beautiful," or "Morning Has Broken"

Gathering Prayer

Leader: God, Maker of all life, Giver of all good things, we gather today to remember and celebrate (Name of child)'s pet, (Name of pet), who is lost. (Child)'s times with (pet) were fun and we are sad because (pet) is missing. We pray that (pet) is safe and we ask that he will be found. We pray, too, that someone will care for him while he is gone. Help us to reflect on the happy times with our pets and to see your goodness every day of our lives. We pray these things in the name of Jesus, who is our friend forever.

ALL: Amen.

Light the candle.

Reading

The next day God turned his attention to the sea. "I want these waters teeming with life," God said. And it was so. In no time at all, there were millions of little fish darting in the shallows, and great monsters patrolling the deep. God made birds, too, that soared through the air, riding the wind and calling to each other. Just then dusk fell over the water, the sky grew dark and the birds and fishes went to sleep. So ended the fifth day of creation.

The next day God said, "Now let me see. We have fish in the sea, birds in the air, and ah, yes— we need creatures on the land." That morning God made all the wild animals: lions and tigers and bears and crocodiles. In the afternoon God made friendlier creatures: cows and sheep and rabbits and cats and dogs. Never was there such variety, from antelopes to ants and from lizards to limpets! "There's still something missing," God said. "Someone to care for it all...someone for me to talk to." And so, God made people.

—Adapted from Genesis 1

Ritual

Cats and dogs, gerbils and hamsters, parakeets and parrots: regardless of the type of creature—animal, rodent, or bird—a missing pet creates mixed emotions. Losing a pet because it flew out of its cage, broke loose from its leash, or escaped from the yard is a traumatic experience. There are feelings of anxiety (Will he ever return?) and guilt (I should have been more careful or held on tighter) as well as joy (We had such fun together) and thankfulness (Thank God for such a special friend).

Acknowledge the fact that (Student)'s pet (Name) is missing. Invite (Student) to show a picture of the pet, to describe what happened, and to share a story of a special time with the animal.

Invite the participants to show the photographs of their pets. If a participant is without a photo, provide paper and markers and offer the person an opportunity to draw a picture of the pet. One by one, invite each person to show a picture and to share a story about a pet. Encourage the pupils to tell the pet's name, when and how they got it, and a favorite memory. At the end of the sharing time, pass a basket and invite the participants to place their pictures in it. Set the basket on the prayer table.

Closing Prayer

Leader: We give thanks this day for all good things, God our Creator.

ALL: We give thanks this day for all good things, God our Creator.

Leader: The day before us is uncertain. We know not what we will encounter on our way.

ALL: We give thanks this day for all good things, God our Creator.

Leader: While we rejoice with those who rejoice, we also weep with those who are sad.

ALL: We give thanks this day for all good things, God our Creator.

Leader: While we may delight in beauty, we may also find darkness.

ALL: We give thanks this day for all good things, God our Creator.

Leader: Wherever we go, we go forth as sons and daughters, servants of the living God, and we go forth to touch the lives of people with your healing love.

ALL: We give thanks this day for all good things, God our Creator.

Leader: Let us begin this day with rejoicing and return to our homes with gladness!

ALL: We give thanks this day for all good things, God our Creator.

Leader: Please join hands and repeat the words of the Lord's Prayer.

Closing Song

Choose from the list given earlier.

ENHANCE

☞ Cover the prayer table with animal themed fabric.

☞ Invite each person to make a list of five (or more) favorite things about a pet. Create a bulletin board display of the projects.

☞ Place a statue of Saint Francis on the prayer table.

EXPAND

☞ Invite a speaker from the Humane Society, a pet refuge, or a veterinarian's office to talk about identification methods and pet care.

☞ Make "missing pet" posters and distribute them throughout the neighborhood.

☞ Refer to the book *Hymn Stories for Children: Resources for Children's Worship* (Wezeman, Phyllis Vos and Anna L. Liechty. Grand Rapids, MI: Kregel Publications, 1995) for a story and activity based on the hymn "All Creatures of Our God and King."

10
Losing Face

EXPLORE

To explore the theme of losing face and to make symbols of unmasking before God and others.

EMPHASIZE

O Lord, you have searched me and known me.

—Psalm 139:1

EXHIBIT

- Candle
- Eye masks in a variety of colors

EQUIPMENT

- Bags (for mask making kits)
- Bible(s)
- Candle
- CD or tape player
- Construction paper pieces (skin and facial feature colors)
- Covering for prayer table
- Crayons or markers
- Eye masks (variety of colors)
- Glue sticks
- Matches
- Music for "You Have Searched Me" (David Haas)
- Paper plates
- Pencils
- Scissors
- Table

Advance Preparation

❋ Display a variety of masks on the prayer table.

❋ Place supplies for the activity in the area where the prayer service will be held.

❋ Prepare a mask-making kit for each participant including one paper plate, construction paper pieces (facial features and skin tones), crayons or markers, a glue stick, and a scissors.

❋ Set the candle and matches on the prayer table.

EXPLAIN

We all want other people to think well of us. We like to be thought of as honest, competent, intelligent, loyal, worthwhile persons. When we do not appear this way to others, or when we believe that others do not see us this way, we experience it as a loss, for which we use the expression "losing face."

Young or old, we do things every day which cause us to lose face in minor ways. Losing face can be minor, such as dropping something and appearing clumsy, or forgetting to do something we had promised to do. Losing face can also be a major loss like being suspended for using drugs or taking a zero for cheating on a test. The intensity of our emotions may be different, but the feeling is the same.

Psalm 139 points out that the God who loves us is the same God who knows us inside and out. He knows our thoughts, our dreams, our fears, the things we say and do when no one is listening or looking. Yet God always loves us. This is good news. And the fact that there can be people who love us in spite or our imperfections, flaws, and incompetencies is good news as well. These people are our friends, those who love us for who we really are.

EXPERIENCE

Gathering Song

"You Have Searched Me"

Gathering Prayer

Leader: God, our loving Creator, you reveal your true self to us through Jesus who became human and walked among us. Help us to reveal our true selves even when we lose face and try to hide our shame. You, God, know everything. You know our needs no matter what mask we put on in front of others or in front of you. Give us the courage today to be honest in whatever we do and to never hide ourselves from you or from one another. We ask this in the name of Jesus. Amen.

Light the candle.

Reading

*O Lord, you have searched me
and known me.
You know when I sit down
and when I rise up;
you know my thoughts
from far away.
Such knowledge
is too wonderful for me;
it is so high that I cannot attain it.*

*Where can I go from your spirit?
Or where can I flee
 from your presence?
If I ascend to heaven,
you are there;
if I make my bed in Sheol,
you are there.
If I take the wings of the morning
and settle at the farthest limits
of the sea,
even there your hand
shall lead me,
and your right hand
shall hold me fast.*

*For it was you who formed
my inward parts;
you knit me together
in my mother's womb.
I praise you, for I am fearfully and
wonderfully made.
Wonderful are your works;
that I know very well.*

How weighty to me
are your thoughts, O God!
How vast is the sum of them!
I try to count them—
they are more than the sand;
I come to the end —
I am still with you.

Search me, O God,
and know my heart;
test me and know my thoughts.
See if there is any wicked way
in me,
and lead me in the way everlasting.

—Psalm 139

Ritual

Distribute the packets containing the mask-making supplies. Invite each student to take out the paper plate and to hold it in front of his or her face. Tell the participants that God knows everything about us regardless of how much we try to hide from God or from other people. We often try to hide to avoid the shame that comes from losing face after doing something embarrassing or something wrong. We lose face when we tell a lie, steal someone else's property, cheat on a test, skip a homework assignment, or give a wrong answer. We lose face when we drop books, slip on the ice, or speak angry words.

Encourage the learners to think of a time they lost face, a time when they wanted to hide because of something they said or did. Direct the learners to use the pencil in the kit and to write a few words about the experience on the back of the paper plate. After several minutes, ask the group to think about ways in which they regained face, for example, instead of telling a lie, telling the truth; instead of taking something that didn't belong to them, returning it to its owner. Teach the young people that in order to unmask in front of others we need to ask for God's help. And the good news is that God will give us the strength we need to right a wrong.

As a symbol of reconciliation and healing, invite the participants to redefine their face. Direct the group to use the art supplies in the packets to create a mask. Encourage the participants to create openings for eyes in order to see and be seen, ears to hear forgiveness, and a mouth to speak the truth. Allow time to construct the masks.

Response

Once the masks are completed, invite the participants to hold them in front of their faces. Offer silent or spoken prayers thanking God for help to regain face or for help to face a difficult situation.

Closing Prayer

Leader: You have looked deep into my heart, Lord, and you know all about me.
ALL: Amen.

Closing Song

"You Have Searched Me"

ENHANCE

✻ Display a book containing photographs of the growth of a baby, while reflecting on the words from Psalm 139, "You knit me in my mother's womb."

✻ Find directions in craft books and create masks from a variety of techniques.

✻ Write heart-shaped poems thanking God for knowing and loving each person.

EXPAND

✻ Create a book of affirmations. Include one page for each person in the class and have the pupils draw or write something positive about each person.

✻ Discuss ways to build up rather than tear down people who have lost face.

✻ Find the word forgiveness in a Bible concordance. Assign each student a text to look up and discover what God's Word has to say about the topic.

11
Broken Promises

EXPLORE

To offer a ritual of healing for those who have experienced broken promises.

EMPHASIZE

Do not worry about anything, but in everything by prayer and supplication with thanksgiving let your requests be made known to God.

—Philippians 4:6

EXHIBIT

- Bible(s)
- Candle
- Clay bowl or pot
- Paper chain

EQUIPMENT

- Candle
- CD or tape player
- Clay bowl or pot
- Construction paper
- Covering for prayer table
- Matches
- Music (see Closing Song)
- Scissors or paper cutter
- Stapler and staples
- Table

Advance Preparation

🕯 Cut construction paper into strips and form them into a paper chain, one link to represent each participant.

🕯 Place supplies for the activity in the area where the prayer service will be held.

🕯 Recruit additional adults to supervise the burning ritual.

🕯 Set the candle, clay bowl or pot, matches, and paper chain on the prayer table.

EXPLAIN

Most of us plan to keep our promises, although sometimes people make promises they never intended to keep. Sometimes we make them so someone will feel better, never stopping to think that they may feel even worse if the promise isn't kept. Sometimes we simply cannot keep our promises, or we may forget that they were ever made.

The Bible is full of broken promises and full of God's faithfulness. Israel was unfaithful many times; nevertheless, God promised them a savior and came through. God understands the pain and loss of a broken promise.

EXPERIENCE

Gathering Prayer

Leader: All good and holy God, we gather for the sake of letting go of promises that have been broken. We come to you all loving God, because you keep your promises. Be with us as we gather to remember and to let go. Give us what we need to heal our brokenness. Because you promise to hear our prayers, we come to you now in the name of Jesus.

ALL: Amen.

Reading

Rejoice in the Lord always; again I will say, Rejoice. Let your gentleness be known to everyone. The Lord is near. Do not worry about anything, but in everything by prayer and supplication with thanksgiving let your requests be made known to God. And the peace of God, which surpasses all understanding, will guard your hearts and your minds in Christ Jesus.

—Philippians 4:4–7

Ritual

Invite the participants to reflect on promises that have been broken, promises they made and didn't keep, and commitments that others pledged and didn't honor. Ask each person to think about one broken promise in particular, one that really stands out in their minds. Offer suggestions such as: has there ever been a time when a friend promised something and didn't do it? Or a time when an adult made a promise and didn't keep it? Has there ever been a time when you said you would do something and you didn't keep your word? Provide an opportunity for discussion of the experiences and the feelings associated with them.

After a few minutes, invite the students to form a circle around the prayer table. Call their attention to the paper strips. When the pieces are linked together they form a chain. If one link is broken (break the chain in the center), the chain is no longer complete. That's how it is when promises are broken. There is a feeling of incompleteness, a feeling of brokenness and pain.

Break the paper chain into separate strips. Tell the participants that they will each receive a piece and that they will have the opportunity to write their broken promise on the paper. Distribute the strips and pencils and suggest that the pupils take a few minutes to record their experiences. Offer guidance and encouragement as the students complete the project.

When everyone has finished the task, again gather the group around the prayer table. Demonstrate burning a paper strip by igniting it with the candle and allowing it to burn in the clay bowl. Allow everyone an opportunity to burn their own broken promise. After each person has had a turn, offer the following prayer.

Closing Prayer

Leader: The Lord keeps his promises.

ALL: The Lord keeps his promises.

Leader: He gives justice to the poor and food to the hungry.

ALL: The Lord keeps his promises.

Leader: He sets all people free and heals all those who hurt.

ALL: The Lord keeps his promises.

Leader: He gives a helping hand to everyone who falls.

ALL: The Lord keeps his promises.

Leader: He loves good people and looks after strangers.

ALL: The Lord keeps His promises.

Leader: Dear God, we burn our broken promises before you as a sign of the hope we have in you, our loving and ever faithful God. We know that some promises are hard to keep, but we also know that you kept the greatest promise that was ever made: you sent Jesus into the world to be our savior. Jesus gave his life so that we might have the promise of everlasting life. Thank you for taking these broken promises and for healing our hurts and our hearts.

ALL: Amen.

Closing Song

End the prayer service by playing tranquil music.

ENHANCE

Ω Display a variety of forms for promises such as baptismal commitments, legal contracts, marriage services, medical oaths, and ordination vows.

Ω Exhibit pictures of the four seasons and read this passage from Genesis 8:22 as one example of God's faithfulness: *As long as the earth endures, seedtime and harvest, cold and heat, summer and winter, day and night, shall not cease.*

Ω Review several prophecies of the Old Testament and their fulfillment in the New Testament, for example, God's promise to send a savior and the realization of this promise in Jesus Christ.

EXPAND

Ω Ask the students to participate in a "prayer partner" program. Encourage each person to remember the partner in prayer at least once a day or to meet periodically to pray for and with each other.

Ω Invite people to make a "promise page" on which they can write down their own promises that were made and those that were kept.

Ω Refer to the prayer service "Promises of God" in the book *Twenty More Prayer Lessons For Children* (Wezeman, Phyllis Vos and Jude Dennis Fournier. Mystic, CT: Twenty-Third Publications, 1997) to reinforce the theme of God's faithfulness.

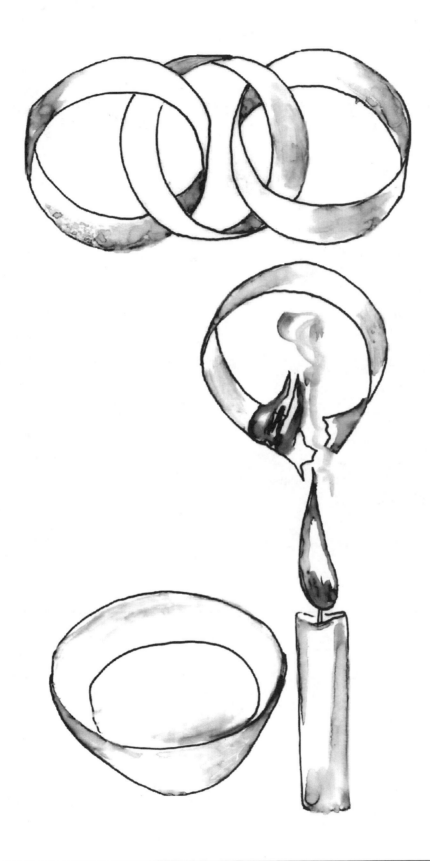

12
Loss of Friendship

EXPLORE

To use the symbols of hands and hearts in a service acknowledging broken relationships.

EMPHASIZE

Beloved, since God loved us so much, we also ought to love one another.
—1 John 4:11

EXHIBIT

• Basket containing paper hearts in a variety of colors
• Candle

EQUIPMENT

• Basket
• Bible(s)
• Candle
• CD or tape player
• Construction paper, various colors
• Covering for prayer table
• Glue sticks
• Matches
• Music for "Of My Hands" (Joe Wise) or "Our Father" (Joe Wise)
• Pattern for hand
• Pattern for heart
• Scissors

• Table

Advance Preparation

♡ Hide paper hands throughout the room (in easy-to-find places).

♡ Place the basket of hearts, candle, and matches on the prayer table.

♡ Place supplies for the activity on or near the prayer table.

♡ Trace and cut at least one paper hand and one paper heart for each participant.

EXPLAIN

When we lose a friend, we hurt. When the loss is our own fault we may also feel guilt. Even if the loss is because of something which has no blame attached, like moving, it is no less painful. Friendships require that people spend time together, sharing their lives with one another, talking about their hopes and dreams. When that is gone, something in us breaks.

Jesus brings healing to those who hurt. He is always present to us and for us. Even though the friend to whom we may have poured out our heart is no longer at our side, Jesus is. He will listen when we pour out our pain and sorrow to him, and he will never leave us or forsake us, no matter what we say or where we go. Jesus will always be our friend!

EXPERIENCE

Gathering Song

"Of My Hands" or "Our Father"

Gathering Prayer

Leader: God of love and mercy, through Jesus, your son, we have been called your friends. Jesus was and continues to be the model of friendship. We gather today to pray for relationships that have been broken, friendships that have ended. We ask you, dear God, to give us strength and a renewed spirit in this time of hurt. Be present within all friendships, so that even in times of anger and confusion, friends will grow in love and care of one another. We ask this of you, in the name of Jesus, who is friend to all.

ALL: Amen.

Light the candle.

Reading

Beloved, let us love one another, because love is from God; everyone who loves is born of God and knows God. Whoever does not love does not know God, for God is love. God's love was revealed among us in this way: God sent his only Son into the world so that we might live through him. In this is love, not that we loved God but that he loved us and sent his son to be the atoning sacrifice for our sins. Beloved, since God loved us so much, we also ought to love one another.

—1 John 4:7–11

Ritual

Gather the participants in a circle around the prayer table. Invite the students to search the room, to locate one "lost" hand, and to return to the group. Explain that the hands symbolize friendships that have been broken, relationships between people that have ended. Sometimes friendships end because people move to other places and they don't see each other anymore. Sometimes friendships end because people have disagreements or are jealous of each other. Sometimes people change and simply grow apart. Jesus teaches us to make peace with other people and to ask for forgiveness from them and from God. Jesus teaches us to love each other.

Tell the learners that they will join the paper hands in an unbroken circle. Invite the group to take turns selecting a heart from the basket, affixing it to the center of a paper hand, and gluing the ends of the hands together to form an unbroken chain. Place the circle of hands on the prayer table. Remind the group that the hands symbolize friendships that have been broken and people who need to be remembered in prayer.

Closing Prayer

Take time to offer silent or spoken prayers for the participants and for other people. Pray that all people will someday be included in the circle of Jesus' friendship.

Closing Song

"Of My Hands" or "Our Father"

ENHANCE

♡ Develop a recipe for friendship. Talk about the ingredients necessary for a successful relationship.

♡ Invite lifelong friends to share experiences with the group.

♡ Read the story of David and Jonathan in 1 Samuel as an example of true friendship.

EXPAND

♡ Create coupon books and give the gift of time together to other people.

♡ Fashion friendship bracelets, pins, or rings and encourage the students to share them with others.

♡ Organize a pen pal project as a way to make new friends.

13
Theft

EXPLORE

To pray with a student who has experienced theft.

EMPHASIZE

To you, O Lord, I lift up my soul.

—Psalm 25:1

EXHIBIT

- Candle
- Large heart

EQUIPMENT

- Bible(s)
- Candle
- CD or tape player
- Construction paper
- Covering for prayer table
- Matches
- Music for "Healer Of Our Every Ill" (Marty Haugen)
- Patterns for hearts (various sizes)
- Pencils
- Scissors
- Table
- Yarn

Advance Preparation

Duplicate the heart pattern.

Place supplies for the activity in the area where the prayer service will be held.

Set the candle, large heart, and matches on the prayer table.

EXPLAIN

Theft affects young people in many ways. School supplies are snatched from desks; lunches are lifted from backpacks; clothing is stolen from lockers. A burglar breaks into a garage and steals a bike or into a home and takes family possessions; a pickpocket grabs a wallet from a purse; a mugger harms someone involved in a hold-up or takes something against another person's will.

Theft involves more than a loss of material possessions. It involves an intangible loss as well—it involves a loss of trust. We may feel vulnerable and violated when something is stolen from us, as well as missing the thing itself. When we experience those kinds of losses we can only be healed by love, not by replacing an object. We can be assured that God still loves us—and can be trusted.

EXPERIENCE

Gathering Song

"Healer Of Our Every Ill"

Gathering Prayer

Leader: We search for you.

ALL: We search for you.

Leader: Heart of God…

ALL: We search for you.

Leader: Healer of our hurts…

ALL: We search for you.

Leader: Joy in times of pain…

ALL: We search for you.

Leader: God of goodness…

ALL: We search for you.

Leader: Hand that shows the way…

ALL: We search for you.

Leader: When all seems lost and without hope…

ALL: We search for you.

Leader: We search for you, God. Remind us of your presence.

ALL: Amen.

Light the candle.

Reading

Truly, O people in Zion, inhabitants of Jerusalem, you shall weep no more. He will surely be gracious to you at the sound of your cry; when he hears it, he will answer you. Though the Lord may give you the bread of adversity and the water of affliction, yet your Teacher will not hide himself any more, but your eyes shall see your Teacher. And when you turn to the right or when you turn to the left, your ears shall hear a word behind you, saying, "This is the way; walk in it."

—Isaiah 30:19–21

Ritual

If someone in the group has had something stolen recently, share appropriate details of the situation. Tell the group that theft is a matter that involves hearts—the heart of the person who stole and the heart of the person from whom something was stolen. One heart broke God's commandment, "You shall not steal" (Exodus 20:15; Deuteronomy 5:19). The other heart is hurt because something important was taken. One heart needs forgiveness; the other heart needs mending.

It is important to remind everyone to respect the property and possessions of others. One way to do this is to learn what Jesus had to say about our hearts. Distribute Bibles and ask volunteers to look up and read passages such as Matthew 6:19–21 and Matthew 22:37–39.

Invite the participants to create a one-string mobile of hearts to symbolize the covenant we have with God and with other people to respect what belongs to someone else. Distribute construction paper—red and various colors—heart patterns, pencils, and scissors. Invite each person to trace and cut out hearts of several sizes.

Letter Scripture verses or key words such as "love" or "honesty" on the other hearts. Assemble a one-string mobile by placing a long piece of yarn vertically on a flat surface and arranging the hearts on it in a line. Place the largest heart at the top and the smallest heart at the bottom. Tape the yarn to the back of each shape. Punch a hole in the center of the top heart and tie a short loop of yarn through it as a hanger. Display the hearts as a way to remember that we are to love God and others.

FRONT

BACK

You shall love Your neighbor as Yourself —Mt 22:39

TRUST

Closing Prayer

Leader: To you, O Lord, I lift up my soul.

ALL: To you, O Lord, I lift up my soul.

Leader: O God, I trust in you; do not let my enemies win over me.

ALL: To you, O Lord, I lift up my soul.

Leader: Let me know your ways, O Lord; teach me your paths.

ALL: To you, O Lord, I lift up my soul.

Leader: Lead me in your truth, and teach me, for you are the God of my salvation.

ALL: To you, O Lord, I lift up my soul.

Leader: Good and upright is the Lord; therefore he instructs sinners in the way. He leads the humble in what is right, and teaches the humble his way.

ALL: To you, O Lord, I lift up my soul.

Leader: Relieve the troubles of my heart, and bring me out of my distress. Forgive all my sins.

ALL: To you, O Lord, I lift up my soul.

Leader: Guard my life, and deliver me, for I take refuge in you.

ALL: To you, O Lord, I lift up my soul. Amen.

ENHANCE

▦ Cover the prayer table with cloth containing heart designs.

▦ Help each student identify two ways to put the summary of the Ten Commandments, Matthew 22:37–39, into practice.

▦ Make puppets and act out the story of the unforgiving servant found in Matthew 18:21–34.

EXPAND

▦ Construct banks and encourage the participants to save for what they want to buy.

▦ Make personalized ID tags and use them to label books and other possessions.

▦ Refer to the "You Shall Not Steal" chapter of the book *Laws To Love By: The Ten Commandments* (Wezeman, Phyllis Vos and Judith Harris Chase. Prescott, AZ: Educational Ministries, Inc., 1996) for additional activities to use to teach this commandment.

14
Living with a Disability

EXPLORE

To acknowledge that some people are born with disabilities and to affirm God's love for everyone.

EMPHASIZE

He said, "Lord, I believe." And he worshiped him.
— John 9:38

EXHIBIT

- Bowl of mud
- Candle

EQUIPMENT

- Bible(s)
- Blindfolds
- Bowl
- Candle
- CD or tape player
- Covering for prayer table
- Matches
- Mud
- Music for "Jesus, the Lord" (Roc O'Connor)
- Table

Advance Preparation

🐚 Fill a bowl with mud and set it on the prayer table.

🐚 Place supplies for the activity in the area where the prayer service will be held.

🐚 Set the candle and matches on the prayer table.

EXPLAIN

Each of comes into the world a unique individual: we are all different. Even identical twins, although born alike, soon develop differences in tastes and interests. All of us have special abilities and talents; but all of us have disabilities of one kind or another as well, in that there are things we can and cannot do. Some people, however, are born with disabilities that make them feel or look different from most other people. They are not able to do things that many others can do. They may feel so different that it seems to them as if they are on the outside, looking in.

The good news that Jesus brings is that he loves us all, and we are all important to him, regardless of what we can or cannot do. He loves us for who we are, his children and friends, not for our abilities, and always considers each person to be of the greatest value. His death and resurrection was for each one of us: that's how much we are worth to him. Jesus doesn't ask what we are able to do; he only asks us to put our faith in him.

EXPERIENCE

Gathering Song

"Jesus, the Lord"

Gathering Prayer

Leader: Merciful and compassionate God, we praise and give thanks for your son, Jesus, who showed your love to all people. We gather in awe at the depth of Jesus' love for you, his Father, and for the great healing that came to the world through this love. Give us the insight and courage to use our talents and gifts to affirm your people.

ALL: Amen.

Light the candle.

Reading

As he walked along, he saw a man blind from birth. His disciples asked him, "Rabbi, who sinned, this man or his parents, that he was born blind?" Jesus answered, "Neither this man nor his parents sinned; he was born blind so that God's works might be revealed in him. We must work the works of him who sent me while it is day; night is coming when no one can work. As long as I am in the world, I am the light of the world." When he had said this, he spat on the ground and made mud with the saliva and spread the mud on the man's eyes, saying to him, "Go, wash in the pool of Siloam" (which means "sent"). Then he went and washed and came back able to see. The neighbors and those who had seen him before as a beggar began to ask, "Is this not the man who used to sit and beg?" Some were saying, "It is he." Others were saying, "No, but it is someone like him." He kept saying, "I am the man." But they kept asking him, "Then how were your eyes opened?" He answered, "The man called Jesus made mud, spread it on my eyes, and said to me, 'Go to Siloam and wash.' Then I went and washed and received my sight." They said to him, "Where is he?" He said, "I do not know."

Jesus heard that they had driven him out, and when he found him, he said, "Do you believe in the Son of Man?" He answered, "And who is he, sir? Tell me, so that I may believe in him." Jesus said to him, "You have seen him, and the one speaking with you is he." He said, "Lord, I believe." And he worshiped him.

—John 9:1–12, 35–38

Ritual

Jesus demonstrated God's love for all people through his words and actions. Jesus told people that God loved them very much—even more than they could ever imagine. Jesus' act of healing the man born blind helped others see that God loves everyone.

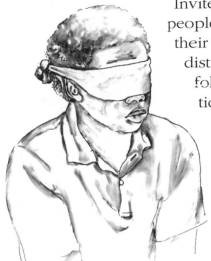

Invite the young people to sit with their eyes closed or distribute a blindfold to each participant. Direct the group to reflect on the story of the man born blind. After a few minutes of sitting in darkness, talk about the different kinds of disabilities with which people are born. Mention that people can be born blind or deaf, some are born without fingers or toes, and others have conditions like Down syndrome or cystic fibrosis; many are disabled by the effects of alcohol or drugs used by their parents.

Remind the students that God loves everyone. Also tell the group that each person—abled and disabled—has the privilege of showing God's love to others. Ask the students to silently reflect on ways that they have been blind to seeing God's love for each person. Also ask them to think of at least one way that they could show God's love to someone born with a disability. Offer examples such as: learn sign language to communicate with a deaf classmate; obtain books on tape for a blind neighbor; locate information about a particular condition. After an appropriate amount of time, ask the participants to remove their blindfolds.

As a sign of commitment to seeing God's love for all and through all people, offer the participants an opportunity to come to the prayer table to place their fingers in the mud and to touch the mud to their eyes. Repeat the phrase "Lord, open my eyes to your love for each person" after each turn.

Closing Song
"Jesus, the Lord"

ENHANCE

🐚 Assign character parts, provide biblical costumes, and dramatize the Scripture passage as it is read.

🐚 Interpret the Bible story through mime.

🐚 Provide clay and offer the opportunity for each participant to sculpt a symbol of God's love for all people.

EXPAND

🐚 Invite a local chapter of "Kids On The Block," an international puppet project that emphasizes special needs, to present a performance.

🐚 Obtain samples of curricula for special needs ministries, including blind and deaf resources.

🐚 Visit a rehabilitation center or invite an occupational or physical therapist to speak to the group.

15
Change of Seasons

EXPLORE

To celebrate the seasons as nature's cycle of change and to affirm God's steadfastness during the changing times of life.

EMPHASIZE

As long as the earth endures, seedtime and harvest, cold and heat, summer and winter, day and night, shall not cease.

—Genesis 8:22

EXHIBIT

- Bowl of seeds
- Candle

EQUIPMENT

- Bible(s)
- Bowl
- Candle
- CD or tape player
- Construction paper
- Covering for prayer table
- Envelopes (small with top flaps)
- Markers
- Matches
- Music for "Praise the Lord, You Heavens" (Jack Miffleton) and "Let Heaven Rejoice" (Bob Dufford)
- Seeds
- Table

Advance Preparation

🎄 Fill a bowl with seeds and place it on the prayer table.

🎄 Make copies of the Gathering Prayer for four readers.

🎄 Place supplies for the activity in the area where the prayer service will be held.

🎄 Prepare seed packets from small envelopes or from construction paper and fill them with seeds.

🎄 Set the candle and matches on the prayer table.

EXPLAIN

When one experiences the seasons changing year after year, each season becomes a smaller and smaller portion of a life. When a person is fifty, a summer is one two-hundredth of his or her life. A child has a different perspective. Each season is a major part of life. To a two year old, that same summer is one-eighth of his or her twenty-four months. A season seems like a much longer time.

The change of seasons can bring real losses. A child who loves to play football may experience a real loss when the season is over. Or a downhill skier may dread the thought of the coming of spring. A child who loves school may feel a sense of loss when summer comes. Time may give us all a different perspective, but even children can be reminded that the God who made the seasons assures us that they will continue to come and go. Each change of season reminds us of the faithfulness of our God.

EXPERIENCE

Gathering Song

"Praise The Lord, You Heavens"

Gathering Prayer

Based on Psalm 148

Leader: Bless the Lord, all you works of the Lord. Praise and exalt God forever.

ALL: Bless the Lord, all you works of the Lord. Praise and exalt God forever.

Reader One: Angels of the Lord, bless the Lord. You heavens, bless the Lord. All you waters above the heavens, bless the Lord. Sun and moon, bless the Lord. Stars of heaven, bless the Lord.

ALL: Bless the Lord, all you works of the Lord. Praise and exalt God forever.

Reader Two: Every shower and dew, bless the Lord. All you winds, bless the Lord. Fire and heat, bless the

Lord. Cold and chill, bless the Lord.

ALL: Bless the Lord, all you works of the Lord. Praise and exalt God forever.

Reader Three: Light and darkness, bless the Lord. Lightning and clouds, bless the Lord. Mountains and hills, bless the Lord. Seas and rivers, bless the Lord. Everything growing from the earth, bless the Lord.

ALL: Bless the Lord, all you works of the Lord. Praise and exalt God forever.

Reader Four: All water creatures, bless the Lord. All you birds of the air, bless the Lord. All you beasts, wild and tame, bless the Lord. You peoples of God, bless the Lord.

ALL: Bless the Lord, all you works of the Lord. Praise and exalt God forever.

Leader: Creator of us all, God of love and mercy, we gather to celebrate the passing of one season and the beginning of another. All of life is given through your goodness. All that lives praises your holy Name. All that continues to be gives you thanks. Help us to be ever mindful of all the beauty and gifts of the seasons: spring, summer, fall and winter. We praise and exalt you above all forever.

ALL: Amen.

Light the candle.

Reading

For as the rain and the snow come down from heaven, and do not return there until they have watered the earth, making it bring forth and sprout, giv-

ing seed to the sower and bread to the eater, so shall my word be that goes out from my mouth; it shall not return to me empty, but it shall accomplish that which I purpose, and succeed in the thing for which I sent it.

—Isaiah 55:10,11

Ritual

Spring, summer, fall, winter: the four seasons. Invite the participants to share their favorite activities for each season, for example taking a nature walk during spring, going to the beach in summer, playing in leaf piles during fall, and making snow angels in the winter.

Recognize that each season brings change, and also loss. Crocuses poke through the ground, bloom, and die when spring turns to summer. Darkness comes earlier and outdoor play time gets shorter as summer becomes fall. Temperatures get colder when fall changes to winter. Seasonal sporting equipment gets stored as winter is replaced by spring.

Explain to the participants that God made the seasons to come and go; God made the seasons to change. Show the group the basket of seeds on the prayer table and note that seeds are a symbol of change, a symbol of the promise of new life. The seed is the part of the plant that contains the life from which a new plant can grow. The God who made seeds is the God who promises us that just as life springs from them, one season leads to another.

Show the students the basket containing the seed packets. Read the words of Genesis 8:22: *As long as the earth endures, seedtime and harvest, cold and heat, summer and winter, day and night, shall not cease.* Pass the basket around the room and have each participant take a package of seeds.

Encourage silent prayer as the basket is passed.

Closing Prayer

Leader: The seed that falls on good ground will yield a fruitful harvest.

ALL: The seed that falls on good ground will yield a fruitful harvest.

Leader: Our God, you take care of the earth and send rain to help the soil grow all kinds of crops. Your rivers never run dry, and in the changing season you prepare the earth.

ALL: The seed that falls on good ground will yield a fruitful harvest.

Leader: Wherever your footsteps touch the earth a rich harvest is gathered. Desert pastures blossom, and the mountains celebrate your seasons.

ALL: The seed that falls on good ground will yield a fruitful harvest.

Leader: Meadows are filled with sheep and goats; valleys overflow with grain and echo with joyful songs.

ALL: The seed that falls on good ground will yield a fruitful harvest.

Closing Song

"Let Heaven Rejoice"

ENHANCE

🌲 As the participants arrive, create four banners representing favorite activities during each season.

🌲 Show photos or slides of spring, summer, fall, and winter scenes as an introduction to the ritual.

🌲 Conclude the service by going outside to plant seeds in the ground or by planting seeds in individual pots for each participant to take home.

EXPAND

🌲 Invite a science teacher or weather forecaster to talk to the group about the equinoxes and solstices that mark the change of seasons.

🌲 Visit a garden center or nature preserve to experience the beauty of God's seasons.

🌲 Write poems or stories describing ways to experience God during each season of the year.

16
End of the School Year

EXPLORE

To respond to the feelings that accompany ending a school year and anticipating a new grade.

EMPHASIZE

Jesus said to his disciples, "Therefore I tell you, do not worry about your life, what you will eat, or about your body, what you will wear."
　　　　　　　　　　—Luke 12:22

EXHIBIT

- Candle
- Report card
- School books

EQUIPMENT

- Bible(s)
- Candle
- CD or tape player
- Construction paper
- Covering for prayer table
- Glue sticks or tape
- Matches
- Music for "Only A Shadow" (Carey Landry)
- Pencils or pens
- Report card(s)
- School books
- Scissors
- Table

Advance Preparation

🕑 Duplicate the End of the School Year Test on page 67, one for each student.

🕑 Place supplies for the activity in the area where the prayer service will be held.

🕑 Set the candle, matches, report card(s) and school books on the prayer table.

EXPLAIN

Changing grades is a time of mixed emotions. While the end of the school year brings the relief of passing marks, the hope of summer fun, and the pride of real accomplishment, it can also be accompanied by feelings of uncertainly about next year's teacher, anxiety about changing buildings, and worry that "best friends" might not be in the same class.

Change is difficult at any age. Adults often forget how difficult it is for children. As one door opens, another closes on some aspect of our lives. It is important to encourage children to look forward to the future as they walk through new doors, but it also important to recognize their loss as old doors close behind them.

EXPERIENCE

Gathering Song

"Only A Shadow"

Gathering Prayer

Leader: God of new beginnings, we stand at the door of another opportunity, an opportunity to change grades, an opportunity to grow and to learn. Help us to know that you are with us at the beginnings and the endings in our lives. We are grateful that you provide for our needs. Help us to never lose sight of that reality. Be with us now as we pray with your son Jesus, who remains forever.

ALL: Amen.

Light the candle.

Reading

Jesus said to his disciples, "Therefore I tell you, do not worry about your life, what you will eat, or about your body, what you will wear. For life is more than food, and the body more than clothing. Consider the ravens: they neither sow nor reap, they have neither storehouse nor barn, and yet God feeds them. Of how much more value are you than the birds!

"And can any of you by worrying add a single hour to your span of life? If then you are not able to do so small

a thing as that, why do you worry about the rest? Consider the lilies, how they grow: they neither toil nor spin; yet I tell you, even Solomon in all his glory was not clothed like one of these. But if God so clothes the grass of the field, which is alive today and tomorrow is thrown into the oven, how much more will he clothe you—you of little faith!

"And do not keep striving for what you are to eat and what you are to drink, and do not keep worrying. For it is the nations of the world that strive after all these things, and your Father knows that you need them. Instead, strive for his kingdom, and these things will be given to you as well."

—Luke 12:22–31

Ritual

As a way to determine how the participants feel about closing one door of their lives and opening a new one, distribute the End of School Year Test (see p. 67). Invite the students to take a few minutes to answer the questions.

Encourage the group to be honest in their responses. When everyone has completed the quiz, organize the students into small groups and allow time to discuss the answers. Encourage conversation about the variety of emotions that accompany changing grades, making new friends, and possibly leaving old friends behind.

Use the theme of opening and closing doors to help the group express their joys and concerns about this stage of their lives. Talk about the doors people walk through in a day or in a week. Doors might include school, classroom, house, garage, bedroom, car, church, movie theater, stores, and restaurants. Also discuss doors that are not as obvious. "Intangible" doors could include deciding to try out for a team, resolving to break a bad habit, or choosing to go somewhere with a friend. Discuss ways that doors can lead to growth and opportunity, even the ones that might seem difficult to open or hard to close.

Provide time for the students to put their thoughts and feelings into words. Place construction paper, scissors, pencils or pens, and glue sticks or tape within sharing distance of the learners. Instruct the pupils to select a sheet of construction paper and to cut a large door-like opening in the piece, leaving a frame in place. Next, tell the group to glue a second sheet of paper to the back of the first piece.

Invite the pupils to write a poem about changing grades behind the open door. Encourage upbeat, positive responses by asking questions such as: What commitments will you make as you move to the next grade? What hopes do you have for the next year? As a guide for the project, suggest that the group follow the formula for a diamond-shaped poem.

Diamond-Shaped Poem

LINE ONE: One or two words that are an opposite of line five.

LINE TWO: Two or three words which describe line one.

LINE THREE: Three to five words which resolve the conflict.

LINE FOUR: Two or three words which describe line five.

LINE FIVE: One or two words that are an opposite of line one.

For example:

Grade Three
Fun and friends
Positive attitude is a plus
Changes and challenges
Grade Four

Encourage the students to hang the project on the door of a room at home and to reread the message as they anticipate a new school year.

Closing Prayer

Have everyone join hands and say the Lord's Prayer.

At the end of the prayer, encourage the children to offer a blessing to each other as a sign of God's love and protection as we open and close the doors of our lives.

ENHANCE

☺ Cover both sides of the classroom door with paper. As the students arrive on the last day of school, invite them to write words or to draw pictures on the outside of the door to represent what they like about the present grade. At the end of class, ask them to place ideas and illustrations on the inside of the door indicating what they look forward to as they enter a new grade.

☺ Obtain a poster of doors or create a collage of door pictures cut from a magazine, and display it on the prayer table.

☺ Place a class picture from the current year or photos from several school years on the prayer table.

EXPAND

☺ Challenge each student to develop a photo essay or to keep a journal of the tangible and intangible doors they encounter in a day.

☺ Encourage each person to create a "time capsule" containing memories of the grade completed and to open it at the end of the next school year.

☺ Take a "field trip" to the new class or school or invite the teacher and students from that grade to come to share with the class.

End of the
School Year Test

Circle "True" or "False" in response to each statement and fill in the blank to complete the sentence.

1. I like being in the _____ grade.   **True or False**

2. I look forward to going into the _____ grade.   **True or False**

3. I think change is exciting.   **True or False**

4. I fear making new friends and being in a new grade/school.   **True or False**

5. I like it when things remain the same.   **True or False**

6. There are many doors for me to open in my life.   **True or False**

7. I always make the best of a new situation.   **True or False**

8. I make friends easily.   **True or False**

9. I find it easy to talk with people I don't know very well.   **True or False**

10. I think school is fun and a good place for me.   **True or False**

11. I will miss my teachers.   **True or False**

12. Saying good-bye is easy for me.   **True or False**

13. Once I walk away from something, I never look back.   **True or False**

14. My best friend is _____; I tell her/him everything.   **True or False**

15. The thing I fear the most about changing grades is

_____.

16. The thing I find most exciting about changing grades is

_____.

Resources

For additional information about the themes and topics developed in **Guiding Children Through Life's Losses**, use the following suggestions to locate print, media and other resources.

Buscaglia, Leo. *The Fall Of Freddie The Leaf: A Story Of Life For All Ages.* Thorofare, NJ: Charles B. Slack, 1982.

Guntzelman, Joan. *Blessed Grieving: Reflections on Life's Losses.* Winona, MN: Saint Mary's Press, 1994.

Hays, Edward. *Prayers For The Domestic Church: A Handbook For Worship In The Home.* Easton, KS: Forest of Peace Books, 1979.

Rathschmidt, Jack, OFM Cap. and Gaynell Bordes Cronin. *Rituals For Home And Parish: Healing And Celebrating Our Families.* New York: Paulist Press, 1996.

Rupp, Joyce. *Praying Our Goodbyes.* Notre Dame, IN: Ave Maria Press, 1988.

Sanford, Doris. *Helping Kids Through Tough Times.* Cincinnati, OH: Standard Publishing, 1995.

—*Please Come Home.* Portland, OR: Multnomah Press, 1985.

Shenk, Sara Wenger. *Why Not Celebrate?* Intercourse, PA: Good Books, 1987.

Most of the music suggested for use with the services contained in this book may be found in the following hymnals:

The Presbyterian Hymnal. Louisville, KY: Presbyterian Publishing Company.

Breaking Bread. Portland, OR: Oregon Catholic Press. Or contact Oregon Catholic Press at 1-800-LITURGY for the music of Bob Dufford, John Foley, Bob Hurd, Michael Joncas, Carey Landry, Jack Miffleton, Roc O'Connor, Dan Schutte, the Monks of Weston Priory, and Joe Wise included in this book.

Gather and *Worship III.* Chicago, IL: GIA Publications. Or contact GIA Publications at 1-800-442-1358 for the music of David Haas and Marty Haugen included in this book.

Of Related Interest

20 Prayer Lessons for Children

PHYLLIS VOS WEZEMAN
AND JUDE DENNIS FOURNIER

Here is a fun and faith-filled guide to teaching prayer. Each simple and direct lesson centers around an activity designed to bring out a particular prayer theme. Activities include drama, dance, games, music, storytelling, and art.

ISBN: 0-89622-689-1, 64 pp, $9.95

20 More Prayer Lessons for Children

PHYLLIS VOS WEZEMAN
AND JUDE DENNIS FOURNIER

Here are 20 more fun and faith-filled ways to teach children to pray. Activities include drama, dance, games, music, storytelling, and art.

ISBN: 0-89622-736-7, 64 pp, $9.95

Bereavement Ministry

A Leader's Resource Manual

HARRIET YOUNG

Here is an all-encompassing resource manual for people who are interested in ministering to those who suffer the loss of a loved one Each session contains clear guidelines for facilitators that include welcoming remarks, the session presentation itself, and a closing prayer. The book also provides several reproducible handouts for participants that can be used during the session or taken home for personal reflection.

ISBN: 0-89622-704-9, 96 pp, $19.95

When Someone Dies

JOANNE PEARRING, EDITOR

This booklet for children takes a loving and warm approach, helping children (and the adults who help them) work through the grief process. In addition to student worksheets there are Scripture readings, a review of funeral customs, symbols associated with death and new life and a description of a funeral liturgy. Full-color illustrations.

ISBN: 0-89622-644-1, 17 pp,
1–9 copies: $1.50 each; 10–24 $1.25 each;
25–49 $1.00 each; 50–99 $.90 each; 100+ $.75 each.

25 Guided Prayer Services for Middle Graders

PAT EGAN DEXTER

This creative, user-friendly prayer service book connects the real-life experiences of children with the words of Scripture. Each service highlights one of the many gifts children have received from God. Topics include the virtues: joy, love, friendship, trust, and forgiveness; physical gifts: hearts that love, and hands that feel and touch; gifts of nature: water, fire, and rock; and spiritual gifts: God's law, suffering, and healing.

ISBN: 0-89622-688-3, 88 pp, $12.95

Reconciliation Services for Children

GWEN COSTELLO

Here is a great aid for teachers and pastors who plan reconciliation services for children. The 18 services help set the tone for children in grades 2–6 to receive the sacrament. Included in each service are appropriate songs, readings, and prayers.

ISBN: 0-89622-516-X, 72 pp, $9.95

Available at religious bookstores or from:

TWENTY-THIRD PUBLICATIONS

A Division of Bayard PO BOX 180 • MYSTIC, CT 06355
1-800-321-0411 • FAX: 1-800-572-0788 • E-MAIL: ttpubs@aol.com
www.twentythirdpublications.com
Call for a free catalog